P9-BZD-793

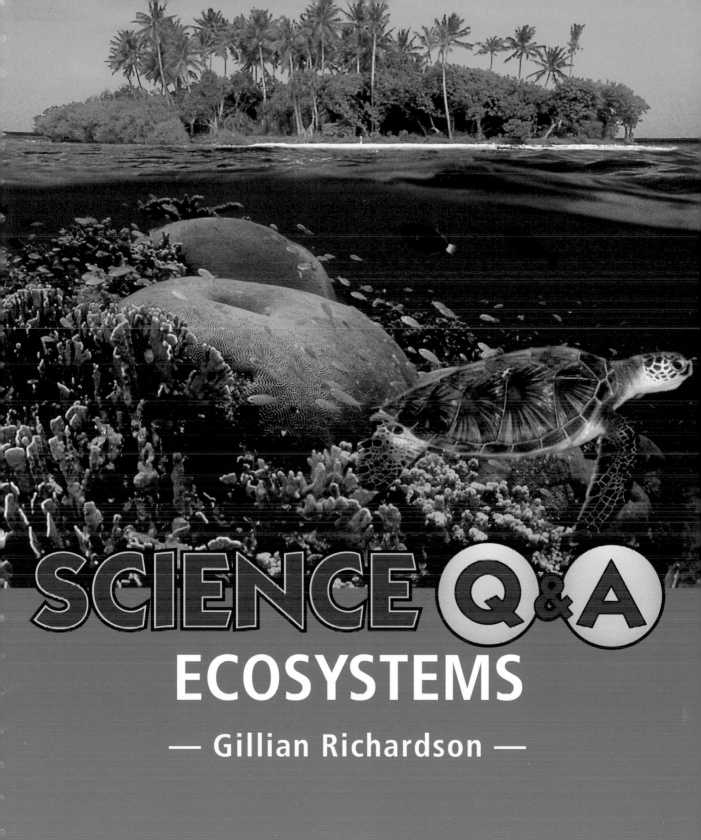

SCIENCE Q&A

ECOSYSTEMS

— Gillian Richardson —

W

Weigl Publishers Inc.

Published by Weigl Publishers Inc.
350 5th Avenue, Suite 3304, PMB 6G
New York, NY 10118-0069

Website: www.weigl.com

Library of Congress Cataloging-in-Publication Data

Richardson, Gillian.
  Ecosystems : Science Q & A / Gillian Richardson.
      p. cm.
  Includes index.
  ISBN 978-1-59036-954-8 (hard cover : alk. paper) -- ISBN 978-1-59036-955-5 (soft cover : alk. paper)
  1. Biotic communities--Miscellanea--Juvenile literature. I. Title.
  QH541.14.R527 2009
  577--dc22

                                2008003820

Printed in the United States of America in North Mankato, Minnesota
2 3 4 5 6 7 8 9 0 12 11 10 09

102009
WEP7000

Project Coordinator
Heather Hudak

Design
Terry Paulhus

Photo credits
All images provided by Getty Images.

CONTENTS

What is an ecosystem?

Have you ever wondered how many animals and plants live on Earth, how humans affect them, and how it all fits together?

An ecosystem is a community of living things sharing a **habitat**. You can think of an ecosystem in terms of a set of dominoes—each piece depends on another piece. When the first piece is pushed over, it knocks over the next, and so on. They all tumble over, one after another. Each **species** in an ecosystem depends on the other species to survive. Whatever happens to one member happens to the whole community. They are interdependent.

Earth is a collection of ecosystems. Scientists are still learning what keeps Earth's large community of living things and its habitats working in balance with each other.

What organisms form an ecosystem?

Life can be found in almost every place on Earth, which can be thought of as one vast ecosystem. Many organisms live in an ecosystem.

An organism is any living thing. Every organism follows a life cycle. It is born, it grows, it reproduces, and it eventually dies. Then, the new generation experiences the life cycle.

Living organisms range in size from creatures that are barely visible through a microscope to gigantic whales and redwood trees. Some animal or plant species exist in numbers too large to count. Others may dwindle to a few individuals or disappear completely. This variety of life is called **biodiversity**. Science helps explain how living things use the same basic **natural resources** of Earth in many different ways.

■ Many species often live in the same area. They must share important resources, such as food and water, in order to survive.

A daisy and a massive blue whale are both organisms. Though the daisy and the whale are both alive, they are very different from each other. Scientists have developed a system, called classification, that sorts organisms based on their differences and similarities. Of the five main kingdoms into which scientists divide organisms, the plant kingdom and the animal kingdom are the most familiar.

Food for thought

It is sometimes helpful to refer to an animal by what it eats. A lion is a mammal, but it is also a carnivore. A carnivore is an animal that eats other animals. Animals that eat only plants are known as herbivores. Some animals, such as humans, eat both plants and meat. They are called omnivores.

How many organisms are there?

So many organisms live on Earth that it is difficult to know how many there are.

Scientists estimate that there are between 10 million and 100 million organisms on Earth. However, they have only identified a small number, about 1.4 million. Even fewer species have been studied. Scientists think they have identified most birds, flowering plants, and large mammals, but smaller creatures, such as **invertebrates**, exist in staggering numbers. It is possible that there are more than 30 million invertebrate species. New species of invertebrates are discovered daily, especially in tropical rain forests, where the greatest variety of plants and animals live.

Over long periods of time, organisms particularly suited to a certain **niche** survived to pass along their traits to future generations. Organisms less suited to the niche died out. This gradual process, called natural selection, resulted in a group of very similar organisms. These organisms share traits that allow them to live and reproduce successfully within their niche. It may take millions of years for a new species to emerge, but natural selection is happening all the time.

■ The deep sea angler fish found its niche at the bottom of the ocean where there is no sunlight. The fish has adapted to this condition. A lure on its head attracts prey by lighting up the dark waters.

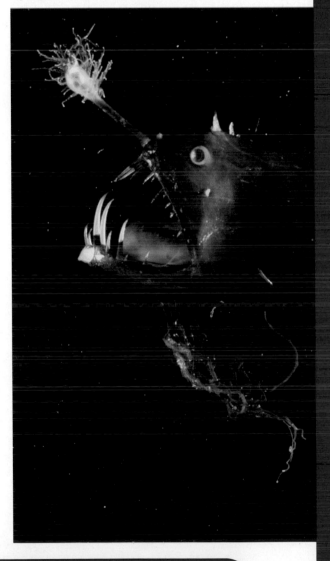

Big bouquet

More than 20,000 types of orchids live in the world's rain forests.

Why is biodiversity important?

With so much biodiversity on Earth, some people might wonder why it matters if some species become **extinct**. Over millions of years, life forms have developed. Many became extinct before scientists were able to learn about them. They are unsure if these species were an important part of the ecosystems in which they lived.

find it quick

Explore Earth's biodiversity by visiting www.amnh.org/ology/biodiversity.

People should care about biodiversity because human beings depend on animals and plants for food. Scientists use the **genetic material** found in certain wild plants to develop new crops that are easier to grow or that produce more food. With each extinct species, important diversity is gone forever.

Many plants provide people with medicines. About one quarter of all prescription drugs have ingredients that come from the natural world.

In addition to its importance to human health, nature improves people's lives in other ways. Humans value nature for its beauty and the enjoyment it brings. Humans create works of art using animals, birds, and flowers as subjects. People visit different places to see rare plant species or unusual wildlife. The diversity that nature offers helps people learn about the past, present, and future.

■ Viewing wildlife in its natural environment can be educational and inspiring.

Healthy plants

Many plants are used to cure diseases and help sick people. Only one percent of the world's plants have been tested for use in medicine.

What are the basic needs for survival?

There are certain things that all organisms need to survive. Although each species may find these necessities in different forms, none can survive without them.

All living things need food, water, shelter, and living space in order to survive. Plants change sunlight, water, and carbon dioxide into food during a process called photosynthesis. Plants use the food to grow flowers, fruit, leaves, and roots. The fruit contains seeds, which will become the next generation of the plant. Animals eat plants to nourish their bodies so they can grow, repair injuries, and produce young.

Some plants require a great deal of water to survive. Water lilies grow with their roots submerged in water. Other plants need little water. Most desert cacti can store water to use during long dry spells. Animals get some water from their food. However, they must have a fresh water supply, such as a river or lake, from which to drink. Some animals need shelter from harsh weather and a place to hibernate during winter. A snug den or nest is required to raise young and provide protection against enemies. Plants also need shelter from extreme climates. Trees do not grow near the North and South Poles because they are too cold and windy for most of the year. Low-growing lichens grow well in these regions.

Living space is important for both animals and plants. In crowded conditions, plant roots cannot develop properly. Animals may not have enough food for all members of an ecosystem.

Here is your challenge!

Clean water is one of the basic needs for all living things. Find out how nature cleans water.

For this experiment, you will need water mixed with soil, a large bowl, a plastic cup, some plastic wrap, and a small pebble.

Place a few inches of muddy water in the bowl, and place the empty cup in the middle of the bowl. Cover the bowl with plastic wrap, making sure it is completely sealed, but not stretched too tight. Place the pebble on the wrap over the cup. The wrap should dip slightly. Finally, set the bowl in direct sunlight for a few hours.

What did you find in the cup? Try this experiment again, placing the bowl in a dark place. What difference do you see?

Where on Earth do organisms live?

Organisms can live in almost any environment. Some rare animals live inside dark caves. They do not need to see, so they have no eyes. Other animals live near vents deep in the oceans. These vents release ultra-hot, poisonous gases from the center of Earth.

find it quick

Learn all about Earth's biomes by visiting **www.mbgnet.net**.

Scientists have categorized Earth's environments into different ecosystems, called biomes. There are land-based and water biomes. Land-based biomes are named for their main plant species, [...] habitats for many living things. The type of plants or vegetation in each area depends on the climate, soil, and elevation. Humans are a factor because people can change these environments and create artificial ones.

The Major Land-Based Biomes

Name	Location	Characteristics
Tropical rain forest	near the equator	dense vegetation, high biodiversity, warm and wet
Temperate forest	areas with cold winters	**deciduous** trees, rich soil, limited number of animal species
Boreal forest, or taiga	areas with short summers located in the Far North	mainly **coniferous** and old-growth trees, furry animals, many birds
Grassland	bordering forest areas	natural grasses, herbivores, alternately dry and wet
Desert	areas typically near the tropics or the North and South Poles	deeply rooted plants, few animals or birds, low rainfall, very hot or very cold
Tundra	in mountains above tree line, around Arctic polar region	low, shallow-rooted plants, cold permafrost, few animals

The Major Water-Based Biomes

Name	Location	Characteristics
Ocean	covers 71 percent of Earth	plants near the surface, varied animal life, saltwater
Inland waters	lakes, ponds, rivers, wetlands	still or flowing water, varied biodiversity, fresh water

How big are ecosystems?

As long as it provides the basic needs for its inhabitants, an ecosystem can be any size.

Earth is the largest known ecosystem, containing countless species and habitats. All of the basic needs for life are found within the atmosphere of our planet.

A single drop of water is an ecosystem for tiny organisms. Nutrients in the water are used for food. Organisms will die if the water is too hot or too cold. For example, humans boil water from some sources because most organisms cannot survive in extremely hot water. This kills harmful bacteria, making the water safe to drink.

A coral reef is an ecosystem found in warm, shallow ocean water. It consists of vast colonies of tiny animals called polyps, which have limestone shells. The reef is a habitat for hundreds of species, including fish, sea anemones, sponges, sea horses, and turtles.

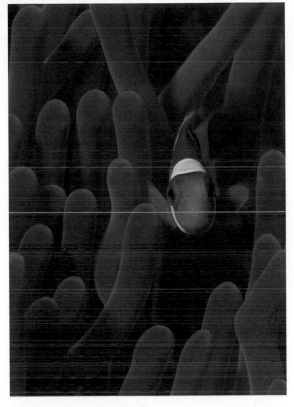

■ Clown fish make their home in a type of polyp called an anemone. The anemone hunts fish by stinging them with a poison barb. Clown fish are resistant to the sting of the anemone, so they can live in safety.

Eye of the taiga

The taiga is Earth's largest land-based ecosystem. The mixture of coniferous and deciduous trees forms a ring around the top of the globe between grasslands and tundra, broken only by areas of ocean.

What is a "suitable environment"?

Humans have adapted to live almost any place on Earth. Many animals, however, need specific conditions in order to survive.

The *eco* in ecosystem comes from a Greek word meaning "house." In English, *eco* means "the place where things live—their environment or habitat." An ecosystem is the space living things call home, and it is one of the basic needs of all life forms. An environment might contain grasslands, mountain slopes, desert sands, or tropical rain forests that are thick with vegetation.

An environment is suitable for life to exist only if the right conditions are present. Earth's environment includes air, soil, and water. Typical weather conditions such as temperature, wind, rainfall, and sunlight determine the environments in which different species are able to survive. For example, a butterfly cannot survive an Arctic winter. A mountain goat prefers steep slopes to avoid predators. Fish cannot exist out of water. A change to the environment will affect the number or kinds of animals and plants living there.

Earth's many environments fit together like a large jigsaw puzzle. Some pieces may be cities, which are artificially created habitats for human beings. Other pieces may be droplets of water, each one providing a home for a certain species of **microorganism**.

Many species need to live in more than one environment. They migrate as the seasons bring lower temperatures that destroy their food supply. They return when conditions are favorable again. Swallows spend the summer in North America and the winter in South America.

■ Swallows can fly a total of 600 miles (965 kilometers) in a single day. This helps the swallow migrate long distances in short periods.

Early bird

An unexpected environmental change, such as sudden cold weather in late spring, can mean death for birds that migrate earlier in the year than other birds. Freezing temperatures kill insects, and without this source of food, birds can starve in just a few days.

How does a balanced ecosystem work?

Earth's ecosystems run like finely tuned machines, with each part depending on the rest to function as expected. A single change can affect the whole system. If the balance is changed in an ecosystem, it can have major effects on all of the individual parts. Scientists investigate the cycles in nature to understand what keeps things in balance. Science provides the tools to restore order when something goes wrong.

find it quick

To build your own balanced ecosystem, visit **www.bellmuseum.org/distancelearning/ prairie/build/tb1.html**.

■ Hummingbirds help flowers reproduce by transferring pollen from one flower to another. A hummingbird can visit as many as 1,000 flowers in a single day.

All organisms in an ecosystem are interdependent. They are connected to each other by their needs. Each living thing uses, or is used by, another living thing. This is nature's way of keeping ecosystems In balance.

Trees use nutrients in the soil to grow. When they die and fall, they decay, and the nutrients are returned to the soil. Many animals use trees. Some spend their entire lives in them. Birds shelter in holes in tree trunks or build nests among branches. They might feed on insects living in the same tree, helping to prevent damage to its leaves or bark. Some insects pollinate, or fertilize, a tree's flowers so that fruit or seeds will be produced. Mammals, such as squirrels, sometimes nest in trees and climb their branches to travel from place to place. While gathering pine cones from coniferous trees, squirrels scatter the seeds. This causes new trees to grow.

The more biodiversity an ecosystem has, the more links there are between its inhabitants. Often these links are related to food through food chains and food webs.

Ants go marching

Ants can be found in all land-based biomes, except Antarctica and a few ocean islands. Biologists have found 43 different species of ants on a single tropical tree.

What happens when an ecosystem changes?

Natural changes to the environment happen often. It may take a long time before humans can see the effects. Gradual change in the temperature and amount of rain may mean fewer plants can grow. Less vegetation means less food and shelter for animals. They must adapt, move to other areas, or die out.

Learn more about volcanoes, and create your own volcanic eruption at **http://kids.discovery. com/games/pompeii/pompeii.html**.

Other kinds of changes, such as a natural disaster, can suddenly disrupt an environment. If vegetation is destroyed by heavy rains, soil can erode. Sometimes, landslides occur. When such changes occur, animals may no longer have the food and shelter they need to survive.

An example of a sudden change in an environment took place in May, 1980, when Mount St. Helens erupted in Washington state. The blast threw thick clouds of ash miles into the air and devastated 230 square miles (595 sq km) of forest. The closest plant life was scorched or buried. Some birds were able to escape. Small mammals were killed immediately or died later because their food, water, and shelter were gone. Some coniferous trees survived because they were protected by late spring snow. They spread their seeds quickly. Roots from burned plants soon created new growth.

As plant life gradually returned, animals moved back to the region. Bird species, such as woodpeckers, used holes in the dead trees as nests. The environment went through an enormous change, but the area was able to stabilize over time, and animal and plant life adapted to the new conditions.

■ The eruption of Mount St. Helens was so powerful that it removed the top 1,306.8 feet (396 meters) of the mountain.

Blown away

A South Pacific volcano, Krakatoa, erupted in 1883. It was the largest eruption in recorded history. The eruption produced so much ash that it caused unusually red sunsets and lower temperatures worldwide for three years.

What is a food chain?

All living things need food for energy. This need links them together like a chain.

find it quick You can learn more by clicking on the Food Chains Movie at **www.kidsknowit.com/interactive-educational-movies**.

Plants are the first link on a food chain. They are called producers because they are able to convert the Sun's energy into a form that animals can use. Plants are eaten by animals, known as primary consumers. These animals are eaten by other animals called secondary consumers. When producers and consumers die, their tissues are broken down by the final link in the food chain, decomposers.

A food chain in the Arctic might begin with microscopic ocean plants called phytoplankton. These tiny organisms take the nutrients they need from the sea. Phytoplankton are eaten by sea-dwelling creatures, such as copepods, tiny relatives of lobsters and crabs. Shrimps called krill eat the copepods. Krill is a favorite food for seals, which are eaten by polar bears. The polar bear is at the top of the food chain, meaning that it has no natural enemies. When the polar bear dies, scavengers and bacteria will consume its body. It will be changed into nutrients, many of which will be washed back into the sea where they will be used by phytoplankton. The food chain has come full circle.

Food Chain

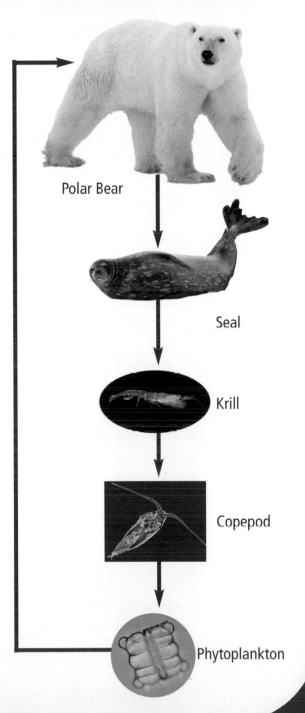

Polar Bear

Seal

Krill

Copepod

Phytoplankton

What is a population cycle?

A cycle is the orderly way events occur in nature. In a cycle, the end of the process leads back to the starting point, much like a circle.

■ Lynx have large feet. These act like snowshoes, allowing the lynx to hunt lighter, faster snowshoe hares in deep snow.

Some animals are so closely linked on a food chain that their population increases and decreases in a regular cycle. Scientists have learned that the lynx and its main prey, the snowshoe hare, follow this kind of population cycle.

Over a period of nine to ten years, hares in a community produce enormous numbers of offspring. This makes hunting easy for the lynx. Soon, the lynx eat so many hares that the number of hares drops. With less of their favorite food available, the number of lynx also drops. When the population of this predator declines, populations of hare begin to rise again. This increase is followed closely by an increase in the lynx population. These cycles continue, and the ecosystem stays in a balanced state.

Son of a gun

Habitat destruction, hunting, or the introduction of a new species can disrupt a population cycle. It can take species years to recover from an imbalance.

What is a keystone species?

While all species in a habitat depend on each other for survival, some species play a more important role in maintaining the quality of the habitat. If these keystone species are removed or disappear from a habitat, the connection between other species in the habitat begins to change.

find it quick

To learn more about sea otters, visit **www.montereybayaquarium.org/efc/otter.asp**. If you are lucky, you might even see some otters on the webcam.

Ⓐ

■ Sea otters are known as the "old men of the sea" because of their white whiskers. The whiskers look like a large white mustache.

Scientists believe some animals, such as the California sea otter, may be a keystone species in an ecosystem. If the keystone is removed, the delicately balanced systems fall apart.

The sea otter is a west coast mammal that lives on floating kelp beds. Its main food is spiny sea urchins from the ocean floor. Prized for its fur, the sea otter was hunted in the 1700s until it was believed to be extinct. Since otters were no longer eating sea urchins, the sea urchin population increased. The urchins ate kelp until it, too, was gone.

Kelp beds provide a habitat for many marine creatures. These creatures are food for fish. Kelp softens the force of waves, keeping the shore from eroding, or washing away, during storms.

Some surviving sea otters were found living farther north along the coast. They were brought back to places from which they had disappeared and were protected by the government. The sea urchin had a predator once again. As sea urchin numbers fell, the kelp began to grow. The natural balance was restored.

The otter side

The sea otter population was once estimated to be at 300,000. When it was finally protected in 1911, only 1,000 to 2,000 remained. Today, it has rebounded to about 150,000 animals.

How long can a species survive?

Not all species remain on Earth forever. Many have vanished since life began on this planet. Scientists estimate that species are disappearing at a rate between about 50 to 135 per day.

find it quick

Find out about endangered species by checking out **http://library.thinkquest. org/06aug/02242**.

An animal population may be at risk if it is very dependent on one thing for survival. For example, the monarch butterfly must lay its eggs on the milkweed plant. It is the only plant species monarch **larvae** can eat. When the larvae are fully grown, they spin their cocoons on the milkweed.

An old-growth forest is a mature, complex, and diverse forest community. It can be made up of birds, herbs, insects, mammals, shrubs, and trees. A seabird called the marbled murrelet nests in old-growth forests, mainly near the west coast of Canada. Scientists are trying to preserve the remaining old-growth forests in order to save the murrelet.

■ Milkweed is poisonous to many animals. When the monarch butterfly eats milkweed, the poison fills its body to protect it from predators.

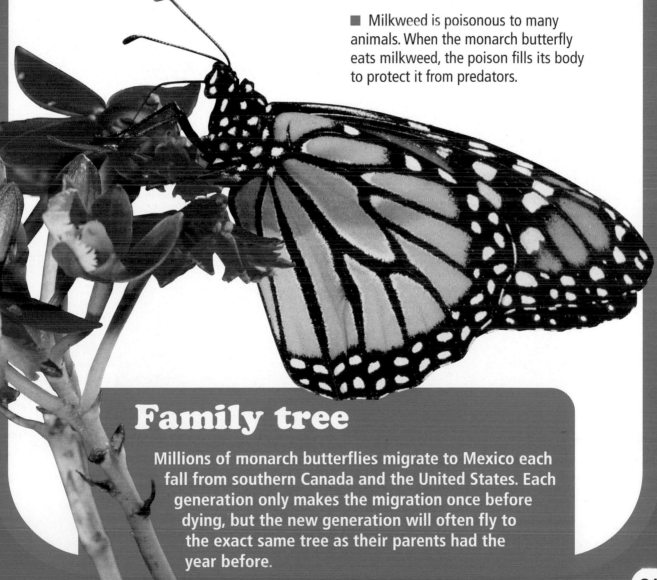

Family tree

Millions of monarch butterflies migrate to Mexico each fall from southern Canada and the United States. Each generation only makes the migration once before dying, but the new generation will often fly to the exact same tree as their parents had the year before.

Can endangered species be saved?

There are thousands of species around the world that are endangered. In some places, they have been completely wiped out. However, they still survive in other places.

Animals can sometimes be returned to a former environment that was disrupted by humans. Wolves were once common in Yellowstone National Park, but hunting and other human activities caused the disappearance of these animals. By the 1930s, there were no wolves left in the western United States.

In 1995, scientists trapped 14 wolves from different packs in Canada. The scientists brought these wolves to Yellowstone, where they were slowly introduced to the surrounding area and to each other. The wolves were kept separately in large pens, and as the

■ At one time, wolves lived throughout North America, Europe, northern Africa, and Asia. Some types of wolves have since become extinct.

scientists studied their individual behaviors, they were placed together in growing packs. These packs proved to be successful in almost all cases.

After being released, the wolf packs moved to different areas of the park. They began hunting and breeding. The reintroduction program has been very successful. Wolves continue to thrive in Yellowstone National Park and in other areas where the same technique has been used.

Road to recovery

The peregrine falcon was listed as endangered in 1970 under the Endangered Species Conservation Act. Thanks to massive recovery programs throughout the country, the bird was taken off the list in 1999. The peregrine falcon's amazing recovery makes it one of the biggest successes under the act.

What impact do humans have on nature?

Every species serves an important function on Earth. From humans to the smallest microorganism, everything has a purpose in the global ecosystem. Humans have found other functions for some species.

find it quick

Play games and see what other kids are doing to protect endangered animals at **www.kidsgowild.com**.

Some human beings use Earth's living resources for profit. Species have become endangered from over-hunting. African elephants are hunted for their ivory tusks, which are used to make items such as jewelry. Alligator skin is prized for purses and shoes. In some cases, human beings have exploited species for food—even to the point of extinction.

At one time, passenger pigeons lived in enormous flocks across North America. They nested in colonies of up to 90 nests in a single tree. Beginning in the 1850s, thousands of these birds were killed by hunters. By the 1880s, the population that once numbered about five billion had fallen to a few hundred. The last passenger pigeon known to exist on Earth was a bird named Martha at the Cincinnati Zoo. Martha died in 1914, marking the end of the species.

■ The ivory trade is illegal, but in Africa, thousands of elephants are killed for their tusks each year.

Here is your challenge!

Find another example of a plant or animal species that is endangered or extinct because of the actions of humans. To learn more about endangered species, try visiting **www.wwf.org** or **www.fws.gov/endangered**.

What is ecotourism?

Tourism to places of natural beauty is a common pastime. It is an important source of income for the people living in the areas that attract visitors. However, large numbers of tourists cause changes to the environments they visit. Resorts built for tourists replace parts of the natural landscape, contribute to pollution, and disrupt animal and plant life.

Over time, many people recognized the problems tourism caused, and they began to develop a new way of traveling called ecotourism. Ecotourism is defined by The International Ecotourism Society (TIES) as "responsible travel to natural areas that conserves the environment and sustains the well-being of local people." Often, the money brought to such areas by ecotourists helps support the endangered ecosystems.

Ecotourists can take a boat tour to see whales during their migration along the west coast of North America. They can also take a safari in an African wildlife preserve, where animals such as elephants and lions are protected from hunters.

The whooping crane is one e[...] of how ecotourism has helped both the species and the local people. This bird spends its winters at a refuge on the coast of Texas. The presence of the cranes draws many tourists and helps keep local store owners in business.

■ Interacting with wildlife, such as whales, [...]ing. However, it can be harmful [...]e and the animals.

The rain forests of Costa Rica in Central America are another ecotourism destination. Visitors spend millions of dollars each year viewing Costa Rican ecosystems. There are rules about where tourists can go and how they should behave to help preserve the rain forests.

Walk in the park

Each year in the United States, 900 million people visit national parks, forests, protected areas, reserves, wildlife refuges, and other places that promote ecotourism.

Are national parks for wildlife or people?

National parks are some of the only places where larger animals can still live in nearly natural conditions. These parks are some of the best places for people to see animals in nature.

find it quick

Learn about challenges wildlife face in national parks at **www.npca.org/ wildlife_protection/threats**.

National parks are natural areas that are protected by the governement. There are more than fifty national parks in the United States. Visitors must follow a set of rules that protect both people and the natural environment. For example, they are not allowed to remove anything from the parks. In order to enter national parks, tourists must pay a fee. This helps the government pay the costs of protecting and preserving the parks.

■ Yellowstone National Park is the oldest national park in the world. It was formed in 1872, under President Ulysses S. Grant.

Many people want more roads built so they can reach remote areas to view wildlife and participate in recreational activities such as camping. Other people support mining and logging in parks to take advantage of natural resources.

Here is your challenge!

Should national parks be kept as natural as possible for the wildlife they protect, or should they be made easier for people to use? Should people take natural resources from parks? Research this issue online or at the library. Make a list of arguments for each side of the issue. Discuss with your parents, teacher, or classmates.

How does human activity affect the environment?

Humans are an important part of many of Earth's ecosystems. They have the ability to change ecosystems more than any other species.

Human activity is responsible for many harmful changes to the environment. Humans turn forests into cities and grasslands into airports, destroying the natural habitats of many other species. Humans fill in wetlands to create more land for crops or buildings. Habitat destruction is a leading cause of the loss of biodiversity.

Use of **fossil fuels**, such as coal, oil, and gas, has led to air pollution, causing a worldwide problem known as global warming. Scientists believe Earth's temperature is increasing. If global warming continues, major environmental changes could occur. For example, the

■ People often spray crops with chemicals that kill insects and other pests. These chemicals can sometimes stay in the crops and harm the humans and animals that eat them.

polar icecaps could melt, causing coastal areas to flood. This is a problem for humans, animals, and plants.

Chemical pollution has increased as the human population has grown. More and more, humans use toxic substances, such as fertilizers, that stay in soil and water for many years. Animals and plants cannot avoid these chemicals in the environment. If the chemicals seep into drinking water, they can harm both humans and animals.

Mouse in the house

Cases of a disease called hantavirus increased in parts of the United States in the early 1990s. It was caused when changes in land use and climate reduced the number of coyotes and other animals that eat rodents. The population of deer mice exploded. Deer mice can be carriers of hantavirus, which can kill humans. Larger numbers of deer mice resulted in more humans getting the virus than ever before as the mice moved into homes and buildings.

What is a rain forest without rain?

For decades, the Amazon rain forest has been getting smaller. Humans are destroying it bit by bit. Trees are cut and burned to make space for cattle ranching or farming. This is how the people living in this area make money. However, the removal of large numbers of trees threatens to destroy this important ecosystem.

find it quick

Visit **www.rainforestheroes.com** to learn more about rain forests. This site offers activities and ideas for saving the world's rain forests.

When a rain forest is left undisturbed, all the parts of the ecosystem work to keep itself in balance. For example, the many trees reflect three percent to ten percent of the Sun's radiation. Their shade cools the air and land beneath them.

As part of the water cycle, water moves from plants to the air. The air is cooled and moistened, and rain falls.

Rain lands on forest tree tops, which slow its trip to the ground. The soil has time to soak up rainfall gradually, providing more water for trees.

When the trees are removed, the air and land become warmer and drier. Less rain falls, but it reaches the ground faster. Soil is washed away with no tree roots to hold it in place. Once nutrients are gone, the remaining soil cannot support plant life. Without plants, animals have no food or shelter. The ecosystem has changed so drastically that it may never be replaced.

■ An area of rain forest the size of a football field is destroyed every second.

Loss of rain forests affects the entire world. There are fewer trees to use carbon dioxide and replace it with the oxygen that organisms need to survive.

Home on the range

Rain forest species can live in an ecosystem the size of a football field. This means that destroying even a small patch of rain forest can potentially wipe out an entire species, not just a few individuals. This is why loss of the rain forests has a much greater effect on biodiversity than similar damage to other types of habitat.

Eco-Careers

Biologist

Biologists may work outdoors in a nature center or zoo, carry out experiments in a lab, or work with museums to help create realistic displays.

Often, biologists focus on one species or environment. For example, marine biologists study ocean life. Ornithologists study birds, entomologists explore the insect world, and botanists deal with plants. Biologists make small changes to the environment, a plant, or an animal so they can observe how it is affected by these changes. A microscope is one of their most useful tools. Computers help to sort out the facts and compare results.

Conservation Officer

A conservation officer's job is to help protect and preserve natural resources, such as wildlife. A key role of a conservation officer is to enforce laws that people who hunt and fish must obey. If a complaint is made against someone who hunts out of season or without a license, the conservation officer investigates, gathers evidence, and may arrest the violators and send them to court.

A conservation officer learns a great deal about wildlife and may assist biologists in the protection of animals. Sometimes, the officer might also be asked to speak to groups interested in the outdoors.

There are many career opportunities involving nature and the environment. Learn about some of these careers at **www.bls.gov/k12/nature.htm**.

Young scientists at work
How does acid rain affect plants in an ecosysem?

Materials:

Two spray bottles

One measuring cup

Distilled water

1 cup (240 milliliters) vinegar

Adhesive labels

Two small, healthy plants of the same size and species

Test:

1. Fill one spray bottle with distilled water, and label it "water."
2. Pour 1 cup (240 mL) each of distilled water and vinegar into the other spray bottle. Label it "acid rain."
3. Label one plant "water" and the other "acid rain." Place them in a warm, sunny window.
4. Every day for three weeks, spray the plant leaves, and keep the soil moist. Use only the water spray bottle on the water plant, and only the acid rain spray bottle on the acid rain plant.

Observations:

What differences do you see between the two plants?

How might acid rain affect a different ecosystem, such as a field of corn?

Take an eco-survey

Your home is a type of ecosystem. Your family is a community of living things depending on each other. Some members work for money to buy food for all to eat. Your house is an artificial environment, but it is still your habitat. It may be easy to forget that you are part of nature. If you take a look around your home, you will find clues about how you and your family fit into a larger ecosystem.

Look into the refrigerator. Do you see food items that come from nature? Can you think of food chains that include you?

Turn on the tap of the sink faucet. What part do you play in the water cycle? Do you know where the water you drink comes from? Where does the water go after your family uses it?

Look in your room. Did any of your furniture come from nature? What about your clothes? Which items are made from artificial materials?

What makes your house a comfortable environment? Do you depend on plants or animals for shelter, warmth, or protection?

POSSIBLE ANSWERS: People may be able to make many of the things they need, but humans are still closely connected with nature. All of our food comes from plants or animals. We use and reuse the same water, as do all other living organisms in the world—there is only one supply for every living thing. Our furniture may come from trees and our clothes from plants and animals. The heat and electricity we use are produced using gas or other fuels found in nature.

46

Fast Facts

Beetles are the largest insect group. About 300,000 species have been identified.

The largest animal group on Earth is insects. It is estimated to include more than one million different species.

The large marine iguanas that inhabit the isolated Galapagos Islands are the world's only lizards that spend time in ocean water. They feed underwater on seaweed and lichens.

Temperatures in tropical rain forests can reach more than 100° Fahrenheit (38° Celsius). The air may be 20° Fahrenheit (7°C) cooler under the canopy of the trees.

A rain forest inhabitant, the emerald tree boa, spends its entire life in the trees, where it waits for its prey.

The soft-bodied hermit crab lives in the discarded shells of other animals.

The Serengeti Plain in Tanzania is home to most of Africa's large mammal species, including lions, giraffes, and wildebeests.

Cockroaches have been on Earth for more than 350 million years. They can live in nearly any habitat and eat almost any food.

Biodiversity increases on all continents near the equator and decreases near the poles.

On the island of Borneo, 1 square mile (0.4 hectare) of rain forest commonly contains more tree species than all of North America.

Glossary

biodiversity: the variety of different species of plants and animals in an environment

coniferous: type of tree that produces cones

deciduous: type of tree with leaves that fall off each year

extinct: no longer existing on Earth

fossil fuels: fuels that come from the ancient remains of plants and animals

genetic material: chemicals in a cell that determine the traits passed from parents to offspring

habitat: the natural environment of an organism

invertebrates: animals that have no backbone

larvae: the immature, wingless, feeding stage of an insect that undergoes complete change to adult form

microorganism: any living thing that is so small it can only be seen using a microscope

natural resources: materials supplied by nature

niche: a unique place occupied by a species in its habitat

species: organisms of the same or similar kind that can breed together to produce offspring that can also breed

Index